R

OTHER WORLDS

OTHER WORLDS
IS THERE LIFE OUT THERE?

by David J. Darling

Illustrated by Jeanette Swofford

DILLON PRESS, INC.   MINNEAPOLIS, MINNESOTA

The photographs are reproduced through the courtesy of the California Institute of Technology; the Cerro Tololo Inter-American Observatory; the Department of the Interior, U.S. Fish and Wildlife Service; the Jet Propulsion Laboratory; the National Aeronautics and Space Administration; and the National Radio Astronomy Observatory, operated by Associated Universities, Inc. under contract with the National Science Foundation.

Dillon Press, Inc., 242 Portland Avenue South
Minneapolis, Minnesota 55415

Printed in the United States of America

Library of Congress Cataloging in Publication Data

Darling, David J.
    Other worlds : is there life out there?

    Bibliography: p.
    Includes index.
    Summary: Examines the evidence which may
support the possibilities of life elsewhere in the
universe and discusses the efforts we have made to
pick up signals from outer space.
    1. Life on other planets—Juvenile literature
[1. Life on other planets]   I. Title.
QB54.D37   1985   574.999   84-23069
ISBN 0-87518-287-9

1   2   3   4   5   6   7   8   9   10   91   90   89   88   87   86   85

Contents

Facts about Other Worlds 7

*Questions and Answers
about Life on Other Worlds*.................... 9

1 The Planet of Life 13
2 Our Neighboring Worlds 21
3 Earth Life and Aliens 29
4 Beyond the Solar System 37
5 Messages from the Stars 43

Appendix A: Discover for Yourself 49

*Appendix B: Amateur Astronomy Groups in the
                United States, Canada, and Great
                Britain* 53

Glossary 54

Suggested Reading 60

Index 62

7/5/85 Olympia 4.95

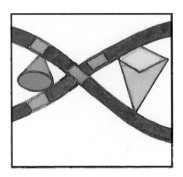

Facts about Other Worlds

Number of Stars: Within our galaxy alone, there are more than 100 billion stars. In all the universe, scientists believe, there may be 100 billion galaxies. The total number of stars, then, may be as many as 10 billion trillion!

Number of Planets: Unknown. Only the nine planets of the solar system are known for sure. Several other stars are thought to have planets, and throughout space, planets may be common.

Nearest Planet: Venus. It comes as close as 24 million miles (38 million kilometers) to Earth.

Nearest Star: The red dwarf, Proxima Centauri, at a distance of 4¼ light-years (25 trillion miles, or 40 trillion kilometers).

Nearest Planet of Another Star: At least two planets are thought to be in orbit around Barnard's Star, less than 6 light-years (34 trillion miles, or 55 trillion kilometers) away.

Life on Other Worlds: Among the worlds of the solar system, Mars, Jupiter, and Jupiter's moon Europa might possibly support life. Beyond the solar system, planets of stars that are like the sun, such as Tau Ceti and Epsilon Eridani, are the most likely home of living things.

Questions & Answers
About Life on Other Worlds

Q. What would alien life look like?

A. We have no idea. If based on the same materials as life on earth, it might not appear terribly strange. If it had come about in a completely different way, though, we may not even recognize it as being alive.

Q. Could Unidentified Flying Objects (UFOs) be space-craft from other worlds?

A. Most UFOs can be explained simply as well-known objects. For example, the planet Venus, unusual clouds, air-craft, or artificial satellites have been called UFOs. The chance that some UFOs might be alien spacecraft is very small indeed.

Q. Will any of our present interstellar probes—*Pioneer 10* and *11* or *Voyager 1* and *2*—pass close to another star?

A. Not for a very long time. One of the first such flybys will be by *Pioneer 10* in the year A.D. 34,593. Even then, it will go no nearer than 3 light-years to the faint red dwarf star, Ross 248—10.3 light-years from earth.

Q. Could there be intelligent life on a planet of the nearest star to the sun?

A. The nearest star of all is Proxima Centauri, a dim red dwarf. Proxima is a member of the Alpha Centauri triple star system, which contains two other, brighter suns orbiting closely about each other. Neither red dwarfs, nor binary (double) stars seem likely to have planets capable of supporting advanced life.

Q. What are some of the problems in searching for radio signals from other civilizations in space?

A. First, such signals would be very faint. It would be difficult to hear them above all the radio "noise" on earth. Second, we do not know at which wavelength, and in which direction, to listen.

Q. What is the most popular wavelength at which to search for extraterrestrial intelligence?

A. Around 21 centimeters—the wavelength of radio waves given off by cold hydrogen in space. Since this natural wavelength would be known throughout the Galaxy, it might be a "standard" for communication among the stars.

Q. What are "Dyson spheres"?
A. Enormous, round shells. Astronomer Freeman Dyson believes such shells have been built by very advanced beings to trap most of the heat and light from their stars. They could possibly be seen from earth because of their strong infrared glow.

Q. What are "Bracewell probes"?
A. Astronomer Ronald Bracewell has suggested that most of the spacecraft sent out by alien races to other stars might simply be robots. Several of these so-called Bracewell probes could even be exploring the solar system at present.

Q. Since so far we have found no other life in space, does this mean that there probably is none?
A. No. There are billions of stars similar to the sun, many of which probably have planets. Our search for alien life has only just begun.

These pictures of six of the planets in our solar system and the earth's moon were taken by NASA spacecraft from several different missions. In the front the earth rises over the moon's surface. The first planet above the moon is Venus; then top left to right, Jupiter, Mercury, Mars, and Saturn.

1 The Planet of Life

The story of *E.T.* is one that we have all heard about or seen in the now famous movie. Could this story come true? Are there really creatures living on other planets far out in space? If so, what do they look like? Will we ever meet one?

In our search for the answers, we begin with a small planet circling around a yellow star. Both are tucked away in the outer parts of a great star city. Both are quite ordinary—except in one very important way. The planet happens to be the earth, our home, and the only world on which we are sure there is life. The star is the sun, our giver of light and heat.

Today, the earth is covered with all kinds of living things. There are creatures in the ground, in the air, in the rivers, lakes, and seas, and even in the soil beneath our feet. Some are so small that they cannot be seen with our eyes alone. Others are tens of feet long and may weigh many tons. There are creatures in all parts of the world, from the snow-blown poles to the dust-swept deserts. But where did they all come from? How did life on earth begin?

These drawings show important changes that took place in the earth's atmosphere. On the left-hand page, water vapor rises and forms clouds that produce rain. The rains caused the oceans to form, and the seas supported the first life on earth. On the

Life In the Making

About 5 **billion*** years ago, the sun was formed from a big cloud of gas and dust that had slowly pulled itself together by **gravity.** Most of the material of the cloud went into making the sun. Afterward, the material that remained circled around the sun as a wide, gassy, dusty pancake.

Over many millions of years, the material in the pancake started to stick together. It formed the planets, as well as smaller objects, such as **moons** and **asteroids.**

Closer to the sun, the newly made worlds were small and rocky. Farther out, they were large and icy. Our world was formed about 4½ billion years ago as a member of the inner group—the third planet out from the sun.

At first the earth was fiery hot, and its body was soft

*Words in **bold type** are explained in the glossary at the end of this book.

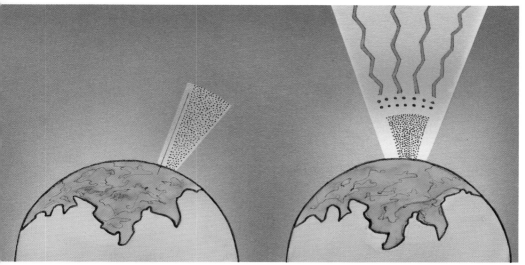

right-hand page, green plants turn carbon dioxide into oxygen. Ultraviolet rays from the sun turn some oxygen into ozone, which forms a layer that protects life on earth from the sun's harmful rays.

and **molten.** Then the rocks at its surface cooled and hardened. Great volcanoes sprang up. Out of these came huge amounts of **carbon dioxide, nitrogen,** other choking gases, and **water vapor.**

At the same time, the earth's surface was being struck by deadly **ultraviolet rays** from the sun. It was not a place that aided the growth of living things.

Slowly, the conditions on our world changed. Because the temperature was right, the water vapor in the **atmosphere** gathered into clouds. Soon it began to rain. Pools of water formed on the ground. Gradually, these grew bigger—and bigger! Finally, they became the oceans that now cover much of the earth's surface.

In the atmosphere above, the sun's ultraviolet rays broke up some of the gases into smaller pieces. These

15

pieces then joined together in new ways. First, they formed simple substances such as **ammonia** and **methane.** Later, they grew into more complicated substances such as sugars and **amino acids.** These gathered as a thick "soup" at the surface of the oceans.

From this strange soup, and aided by ultraviolet rays and lightning, the important materials needed for life were made. Some were broken up almost as soon as they were formed. Others lasted longer and had the chance to grow or change.

About 3½ billion years ago, substances called **proteins** and **nucleic acids** appeared. These clung to each other in different ways. In time, "bags" of protein and nucleic acid came together that could make copies of themselves. These were the first living things, and the thick

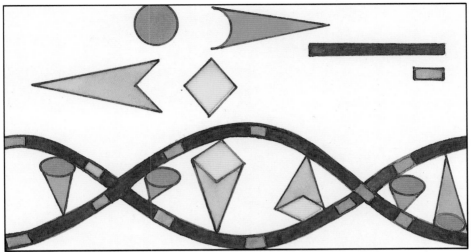

This drawing shows the parts of a group of nucleic acids known as DNA (deoxyribo-nucleic acid). DNA molecules in the nuclei of cells are the basis for passing on the characteristics of one generation of living things to another. Above are the six parts of DNA and a cross-section from a DNA molecule.

soup that surrounded them became their food.

Plants and Animals

Next, from gases broken up by the sun's ultraviolet rays, a layer of **ozone** formed high in the atmosphere. This layer worked like an umbrella, stopping any more ultraviolet rays from reaching the surface.

Back in the ocean, it allowed the first tiny plants to appear. These could now use the safe light from the sun to supply their own energy needs. At the same time, they began turning carbon dioxide in the atmosphere into **oxygen.**

Millions of years later, the first animals appeared in the oceans. Using gills, they breathed the oxygen, made by plants, from the surrounding seawater. In time some of

17

After the oceans formed and a protective layer of ozone took shape high in the atmosphere, life developed in the oceans and moved onto land. The golden eagle (above) and the pronghorned antelope (above right) are two examples of the magnificent creatures now found on earth.

18

them began crawling out onto the land. Then, slowly, these animals developed lungs so that they could breathe oxygen straight from the air.

Wherever life went on the earth, it changed to suit its surroundings. Each animal and plant found its own place and its own way of getting food so that it could best survive.

Several **million** years ago, the first animals appeared that looked something like the people of the world today. Gradually, they learned to use tools and fire, and to raise animals and crops. They became the most intelligent living things of all—humans.

APOLLO ASTRONAUTS GO FOR A DRIVE ON THE MOON IN THE LUNAR ROVER

2 Our Neighboring Worlds

Could the same things that led to life on earth have happened on other worlds, too? Is there really life "out there"? In our search for the answers, we shall begin close to home and then move steadily outwards to greater and greater distances.

The Kingdom of the Sun

Closest to earth are all the other objects that make up the sun's kingdom, the **solar system.** These include the sun itself, at a distance of 93 million miles (150 million kilometers), and the earth's eight neighboring planets. They also include the moons of the planets and countless small objects such as asteroids, comets, and meteors.

In recent years scientists have learned a great deal about the nearby worlds of the solar system. Astronomers have studied them through giant telescopes. The United States and the Soviet Union have begun to explore many of them with spacecraft.

The Moon

At a distance of just 238,900 miles (384,400 kilometers), the moon is easily our nearest neighbor in space. But it has no water, no air, no atmosphere of any kind. During

This photograph of Mercury's surface was taken by *Mariner 10* from a distance of 3,700 miles (5,900 kilometers). Many craters dot the hot, lifeless surface of the planet closest to the sun.

the day, its surface is very hot. At night, it is very cold.

So far the moon is the only world, beyond the earth, that humans have visited. It was the target of the Apollo missions. At first, great care was taken when each Apollo spacecraft returned in case dangerous "moon bugs" had been picked up during the mission. But soon it became clear that nothing had ever lived in the lunar rocks. The moon, as expected, was a dead place.

Mercury and Venus

Just 36 million miles (58 million kilometers) from the sun is tiny Mercury. Pictures sent back by *Mariner 10* have shown it to be a world much like the moon—scarred by craters, ridges, cracks, and mountains. It has no atmosphere, no water, and terrible extremes of heat and

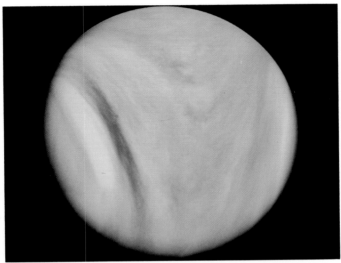

On February 10, 1979, the *Pioneer-Venus Orbiter* took this picture of cloud-covered Venus. The planet's surface is always hidden beneath a thick layer of dense clouds.

cold. Mercury, too, must be a lifeless planet.

Its neighbor, Venus, is almost twice as far from the sun. Years ago, some scientists thought that the surface of Venus might have steaming jungles—as our own planet had before the Age of the Dinosaurs. Others believed that it might be covered by a great ocean in which there could be all kinds of strange creatures.

Now we have a very different picture. Our spacecraft have shown us that Venus is an even more dangerous place than Mercury! In fact, due to its thick carbon dioxide atmosphere—trapping the sun's heat in the same way as a greenhouse—it is the hottest planet of all. Day and night, its surface sizzles at 864°F (462°C).

Nothing could live in such a fiery place. Yet, in many ways, Venus is a planet much like our own. Its size and rocky makeup are about the same as earth's. It even went through a similar period, long ago, when volcanoes erupted across its surface.

The big difference is that Venus is more than 20 million miles closer to the sun. At this distance, it is too hot for clouds of water vapor to fall as rain. Since oceans could never form, Venus lacked a birthplace for life. Without plants, its thick carbon dioxide atmosphere could not be turned into oxygen, and it remains unchanged to this day.

Mars

Of all the worlds in the solar system, Mars has seemed to offer the best hope for life beyond the earth. At a distance of 141 million miles (228 million kilometers)

A camera on board *Viking 2* took this photograph of a field of Martian boulders stretching nearly two miles (three kilometers) out from the spacecraft.

from the sun, it is a colder planet than our own. Yet, it is perhaps not too cold for life to exist.

Around the turn of this century, astronomers reported seeing lines running across the face of Mars. These were thought by some to be channels or canals. The American astronomer, Percival Lowell, believed they had been built by a race of Martians to carry water from the poles of the planet to its drier regions!

It was a wonderful idea. But today, our spacecraft have shown it to be quite wrong. There are no canals and, as far as we know, there are no Martians either.

The gravity of Mars is too weak for it to have held on to a dense atmosphere. What's more, all of the Martian water appears to be completely frozen—either at the poles or deep underground.

In 1976, two Viking **probes** arrived on Mars. They were the first spacecraft ever to land on another planet to make a search for life. Both tested the Martian soil. The Viking probes also sampled the atmosphere and sent back pictures of the red, rock-strewn deserts around them. But neither spacecraft found any trace of living things.

There may be life on other parts of Mars that we haven't yet explored. Pictures taken from space have shown that the planet once had running water. Long ago, it had a thicker atmosphere, too. As a result, there's just a chance that Martian life may have developed in the distant past. If this is the case, it may still survive today in places that are not too cold or dry. Only future spacecraft will give us the answer.

Saturn, an outer planet, and its many rings, photographed by *Voyager 2*.

The Outer Planets

Beyond Mars and the inner parts of the solar system, the planets change. Rather than balls of rock, they are huge balls of frozen gases—mostly **hydrogen, helium,** methane, and ammonia.

Because they receive little sunlight, the outer planets are extremely cold. At their cloud tops, their temperatures range from about –240°F (–150°C), in the case of Jupiter, to about –400°F (–240°C), in the case of lonely Pluto. These icy giants cannot support living things such as we find on Earth. As we have seen, the special conditions on Earth made life as we know it possible.

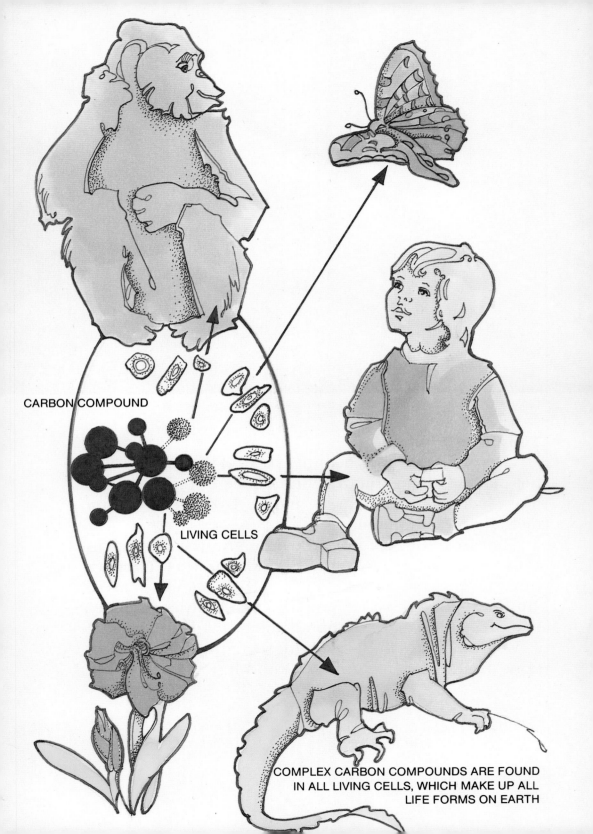

CARBON COMPOUND

LIVING CELLS

COMPLEX CARBON COMPOUNDS ARE FOUND
IN ALL LIVING CELLS, WHICH MAKE UP ALL
LIFE FORMS ON EARTH

3 Earth Life and Aliens

Look around the earth and you will find an amazing variety of living things. What could be more different than an eagle and a centipede, or an elephant and a cactus? Yet, all life on this planet shares a number of important things in common.

First, whether animal or plant, each living thing is made of tiny parts called **cells.** The simplest living things, such as germs, have just one cell. The most complicated ones, such as people, have billions of cells.

Second, all life on earth contains, within its cells, proteins and nucleic acids. These are its basic building blocks—the substances that make animals and plants different from nonliving things.

Third, proteins, nucleic acids, and other materials important to life contain **carbon.** Nothing is better than carbon at joining together to make bigger or more complicated substances.

The smallest parts of people are almost exactly the same as the smallest parts of whales, or of tulips, or of any other animal or plant on earth. Scientists say all living things are so much alike because they have developed from the same starting point. Researchers have traced all life on this planet back to the first simple living things that formed in the oceans billions of years ago.

Because they developed from the same ancestors, living things are alike in other ways, too. All life has adapted to the conditions on the earth—its temperature, atmosphere, gravity, amount of sunlight, and so on. Every animal and plant would find it hard to live anywhere away from our planet.

But does a planet have to be just like the earth for it to have living things? Could there be life on worlds quite different from ours?

Other Worlds, Other Life

Scientists have argued for years about what life in other parts of the universe might be like. There are those who believe that living things everywhere must be built

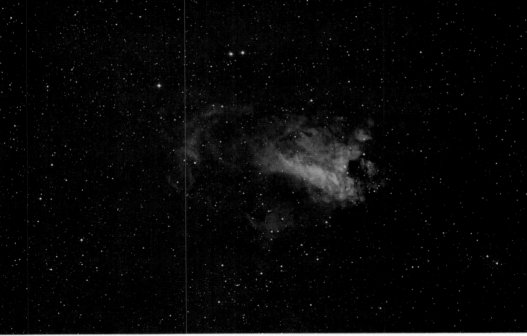

The Omega nebula in the constellation of Sagittarius is an example of the type of bright nebula—a concentration of gas and dust in space—in which molecular clouds are often found. Simple carbon substances have been discovered in these great clouds far out in space.

from proteins and nucleic acids, just as they are on earth. There are others who think that this is too narrow a view.

It has been suggested that alien life could be based, not on carbon, but on **silicon** or even ammonia. Other ideas are for strange life forms made of clouds of gas or pure energy. Until we find just one example of alien life, though, we simply won't know.

At present, most scientists would agree that carbon seems to be the best material from which to build life. Simple carbon substances have been discovered far out in space. They occur in the great **molecular clouds** where most new stars are formed.

Closer to home, **meteorites**—bits and pieces left over from the making of the solar system—crash into the earth. Some, of a type called **carbonaceous chondrite,** are

31

among the oldest rocks known. These meteorites have been shown to contain amino acids.

Such discoveries suggest that life elsewhere may be made along the same lines as it is here on earth. Given the right place, simple carbon substances may often grow into proteins, nucleic acids—and life. But where is the right place? On what other worlds might we expect life to occur?

Within our own solar system, we have already ruled out the moon, Mercury, and Venus as being either too hot or without an atmosphere. Mars, too, appears dead. In fact, of all the inner planets, only Earth is at just the right distance from the sun to be able to support life easily. Farther away, though, the icy giants of the outer solar system deserve a closer look.

Jupiter is the largest planet in the solar system. Its atmosphere contains the same gases that once surrounded earth—methane, ammonia, hydrogen—and water vapor at the warmer levels.

Beneath Clouds and Seas

Moving around the sun at a distance of 484 million miles (778 million kilometers), is Jupiter, the largest planet. Because it receives much less sunlight than Earth, its topmost cloud layers are very cold.

Pulled inward by its own gravity, Jupiter is still shrinking billions of years after it was formed. This inward pull causes heat to flow outwards from the middle of the planet. As a result, Jupiter's atmosphere, just a few hundred miles below the cloud tops, is as warm as a sunny summer day on Earth!

The giant planet's atmosphere contains the same gases that once surrounded Earth: methane, ammonia, and hydrogen. At the warmer levels, there is water vapor. Throughout the atmosphere, great lightning bolts crackle.

Taken from more than a million miles away, this *Voyager 1* photograph shows Jupiter's Great Red Spot. The Great Red Spot is an enormous, centuries-old cyclone.

Given these conditions, life could have formed on Jupiter in the same way that it did on Earth. The big difference is that it would have formed in the atmosphere rather than in an ocean or on a hard surface.

Today, if there are living things in the warmer parts of Jupiter, they are probably very small and simple. On the other hand, there is just a chance that larger creatures live there. Perhaps, as some scientists have suggested, strange balloonlike beasts may float among the orange and red clouds of the great planet.

It is also possible that there is life on Europa, one of Jupiter's moons. Pictures sent back by the Voyager spacecraft have shown Europa to be like an enormous cracked marble. Its frozen surface is as smooth as any of the known worlds in the solar system. Yet, beneath this icy

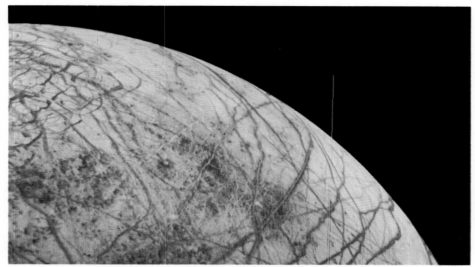
During its closest approach to Europa, *Voyager 2* took this photo of its cracked, marblelike surface. Scientists believe that living things may have developed long ago in its seas.

coating, scientists think there may be a vast, deep ocean of water.

Long ago, when Europa was warmed by heat from the newly formed Jupiter, living things may have developed in its seas. If so, they may still be there today. We won't know for sure until spacecraft land on Europa's strange surface and peer into the dark oceans below.

The other worlds in the outer solar system are all bitterly cold. Yet some of them may have more sheltered, warmer parts where life exists.

Outside the sun's kingdom are billions of strange, unknown worlds. Many of them offer exciting possibilities for finding new life forms.

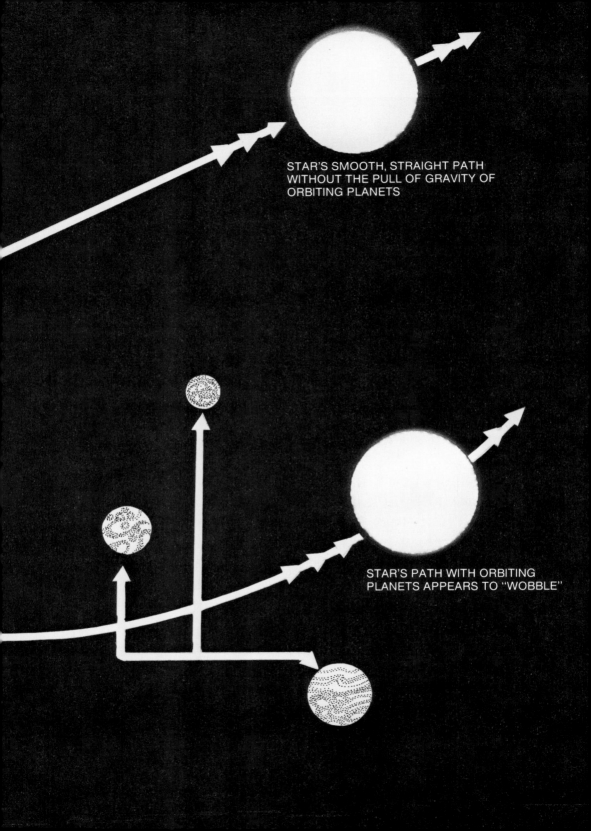

STAR'S SMOOTH, STRAIGHT PATH
WITHOUT THE PULL OF GRAVITY OF
ORBITING PLANETS

STAR'S PATH WITH ORBITING
PLANETS APPEARS TO "WOBBLE"

4 Beyond the Solar System

Imagine that you could travel to one of the nearest stars and then look back on our own sun. The sun, from so far away, would be just another tiny point of light in the sky. What's more, it would appear to be alone. You would not be able to spot any of the planets that go around it through even the largest of telescopes.

For the same reason, we cannot, from earth, see other worlds around other stars. How, then, can we find out if they are there? This is the first question we must answer in our search for life beyond the solar system.

Hunting for New Worlds

If a star is completely alone, then it will move through space along a smooth, straight path. But if, like the sun, it has planets, then its path will "wobble." It does so because it is being tugged, ever so slightly, by the gravity of its surrounding worlds.

Astronomers now believe they have found such wobbles in the paths of several nearby stars. These include Barnard's Star, 61 Cygni, Tau Ceti, and Epsilon Eridani. All are within a distance of 12 **light-years,** or about 70 **trillion** miles. That makes them very close compared with most objects outside the solar system.

The Infrared Astronomy Satellite (IRAS) has discovered what may be planets in the making—thick clouds of gas and dust around several stars. In the drawing above, a gas and dust cloud surrounds Vega, one of the stars studied by IRAS.

Other evidence for planets has come recently from the Infrared Astronomy Satellite (IRAS). Designed to explore the vast, faraway areas of space, it was launched in 1983. IRAS has found what may be planets in the making—thick clouds of gas and dust surrounding several stars, including Vega, Formalhaut, and Beta Pictoris.

In 1984 Arizona scientists discovered a strange object circling around the faint star, Van Biesbroeck 8. About 21 light-years from Earth, the object, named VB 8B, is thought to be roughly the size of Jupiter, but 30 to 80 times as heavy. It has a surface temperature of 2,000°F (1,100°C). Seemingly part-star, part-planet, it may be a "brown dwarf"—an object that never became quite heavy enough to shine on its own.

Since we live within a universe of enormous size,

In this picture, an artist imagines what the surface of a planet around a faraway star might be like. Here strange, gaseous life forms reproduce by dividing into smaller life forms of the same kind.

there may be countless other planets outside our own solar system. The **Galaxy,** the star city in which we live, contains more than 100 billion stars. And throughout space, scientists believe there may be as many as 100 billion **galaxies!** It is likely, then, that somewhere among the stars life—perhaps intelligent life—exists.

Strange Possibilities

Many stars in our galaxy are like the sun. Tau Ceti and Epsilon Eridani are two of the closest examples. These are stars that are neither very hot, nor very cool; neither very big, nor very small. If they have planets at just the right distance, as the earth is from the sun, then they may support life.

A very large number of stars, though, are not like the

This is an artist's view of an imaginary civilization with advanced technology on a world circling a binary star. The star is smaller than Jupiter and gives off only as much light as the full moon.

40

sun. Among these are the dim **red dwarfs; giants** and **supergiants,** both hot and cool; stars that change their brightness; even stars that circle around each other.

Imagine living on a planet with two or more suns in the sky, perhaps of different sizes and colors. Picture making your home around a star that's smaller than Jupiter and gives only as much light as the full moon. We can only guess what life would be like on such a world.

Most stars, even if they have planets, may not be able to support life. Some may have worlds on which there is only very simple life—perhaps plants or tiny animals. But a few may have the right conditions for living things that, like ourselves, are far more advanced. There may, in fact, be great races of intelligent beings in other parts of the Galaxy. Already, scientists have tried to find them.

RADIO TELESCOPES AT THE NATIONAL RADIO ASTRONOMY OBSERVATORY IN
GREEN BANK, WEST VIRGINIA HAVE BEEN USED TO SEARCH FOR MESSAGES

5 Messages From the Stars

In 1960, astronomer Frank Drake began the first real search for intelligent life beyond the solar system. He chose as his target two of the nearest sunlike stars that are thought to have planets: Tau Ceti and Epsilon Eridani. Drake listened for radio signals that might be coming from these stars, but found nothing.

Since then, other scientists have looked for messages from the stars. They have aimed their giant **radio telescopes** at individual stars, at clusters of stars, and even at entire galaxies. No signals from an intelligent alien race have been found so far.

The number of stars on which there could be intelligent life—even in our own galaxy—is enormous. The range of possible signals is huge, too. For example, what type, or **wavelength,** of radio waves should we look for? Could signals be coming to us in some other form—perhaps as ultraviolet rays or as **X rays**? Our search for messages from space has only just begun.

Meanwhile, on earth, we are busy sending out signals of our own. Since the earliest days of radio, and later of television, our newscasts, music, comedy shows, and sports broadcasts have been traveling out into space at the speed of light. By now, the first of them will have reached a dis-

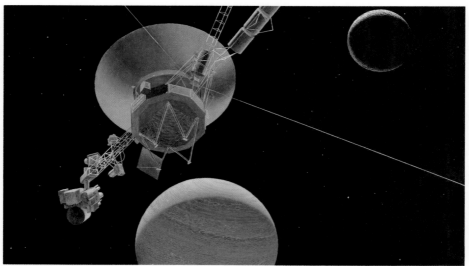

In this picture *Voyager 2* observes Neptune after passing by on its way out of the solar system. If all goes according to schedule, *Voyager 2* will pass by Neptune in August 1989.

tance of about 70 light-years from the earth. They will have passed by many other stars. If they have been picked up by an intelligent race, we can only wonder what the aliens will think of us. Perhaps, in time, they will try to reply.

Not only our radio signals, but also some of our spacecraft are traveling to the stars. Already, four probes—*Pioneer 10* and *11* and *Voyager 1* and *2*—are on their way out of the solar system. We have no idea what will happen to them. But in case they are ever found by other living things, they carry messages telling about our world and solar system.

Pioneer 10 bears a simple gold-plated aluminum plaque with a picture of a man and a woman, a chart of the solar system, and some information about the sun and its planets. The Voyager craft both carry records

In the twenty-first century, space colonies such as the one shown in this artist's drawing may be home for thousands of people from earth. As our own technology advances, we will be searching for signs of intelligent life elsewhere.

which, if properly played, will show pictures of the earth and give greetings from its people.

It is possible that alien races have also sent their spacecraft to us. Robot probes from other stars may already be exploring the solar system. Perhaps in the years to come we shall find them.

It is also possible that we will discover intelligent life that is much more advanced than ourselves. The American scientist, Freeman Dyson, has said that advanced beings might try to capture most of the light and heat from their star by surrounding it with a huge, round shell. This system would provide an almost limitless supply of energy. At the same time, the shell would block out the star's light but would itself give off **infrared rays** —a tell-tale glow that we might see from earth.

In this photo of a cluster of galaxies in the constellation of Centaurus, each galaxy visible contains more than 100 billion stars. So many stars, and probably planets, exist that scientists believe that someday we will find alien life.

Radio telescopes such as this one in Greenbank, West Virginia, are equipped to receive signals from intelligent life far away from earth.

Today we do not know when the first signs of alien life will be found. It may be 20 years from now, when an astronaut or cosmonaut discovers lichen growing near the frosty foot of a Martian volcano. It may be in 50 years, when we stumble across a crashed alien probe on the methane wastelands of Pluto. Or, it may be tomorrow, when a message from another star appears on the read-out of a radio telescope.

Right now we cannot even be sure if there is life out there. If there is, and we find it, then everyone may benefit from the discovery. Yet, if it turns out that we are alone, then we also will gain important knowledge. We shall realize what a precious place our own earth is, the only home of living things in the universe.

Appendix A:
Discover For Yourself

1. *Design an Alien World*

To begin with, choose the type of star your alien world will orbit. There are many possibilities: a star similar to the sun; a red giant; a white or red dwarf; perhaps even a binary star. Using this and other books on astronomy as guides, decide how hot your star will be and how big and bright. Write all these details down in a special notebook.

Next, place your imaginary world in an orbit about the star. What is the size and shape of the orbit? It may be especially complicated if there is more than one star. How will the orbit affect the amount of light and heat the planet receives?

Now decide upon the length of the planet's day (how fast it spins) and upon the tilt of the axis. Write down the size of your world and what it is made of. Build an atmosphere by choosing which gases, and how much of each, there will be. Draw pictures of the planet showing its oceans, land masses, and polar ice caps. Describe what you think it might be like on the surface: its weather, seasons, and so on. How would the star you have chosen appear in the planet's sky? Would there be any moons or rings on view?

Finally, decide if any life would be possible on the world you have made. If so, how would it have adapted to the planet's atmosphere, temperature, and other conditions? Draw a picture of your alien beings. Are they intelligent? Have they built cities, or perhaps even spacecraft for traveling to other stars?

2. *Hold a Classroom Debate*

Choose a title for the debate; for example: *Is There Other Life in the Universe*? Elect a chairperson and six panel members. Three from this team might argue the case for alien life, and the other three might present the case against it. The rest of the class would make up the audience and would be able to ask questions or express opinions.

The chairperson should have a list of key points for debate. These might include:

- How many other planets in the Galaxy support life?
- What are the chances of finding intelligent life on other worlds?
- If other intelligent races exist, why haven't they tried to contact us?
- Should we be trying harder to search for alien signals?
- What would happen if we found other life in space?
- What would we do if that life were more advanced than ourselves?

Appendix B:
Amateur Astronomy Groups
in the United States,
Canada, and Great Britain

For information or resource materials about the subjects covered in this book, contact your local astronomy group, science museum, or planetarium. You may also write to one of the national amateur astronomy groups listed below.

United States

The Astronomical League
Donald Archer,
   Executive Secretary
P.O. Box 12821
Tucson, Arizona 85732

American Association of
   Variable Star Astronomers
187 Concord Avenue
Cambridge, Massachusetts 02138

Great Britain

Junior Astronomical Society
58 Vaughan Gardens
Ilford
Essex IG1 3PD England

British Astronomical Assoc.
Burlington House
Piccadilly
London W1V 0NL England

Canada

The Royal Astronomical Society of Canada
La Société Royale d'Astronomie du Canada
Rosemary Freeman, Executive Secretary
136 Dupont Street
Toronto, Ontario M5R 1V2

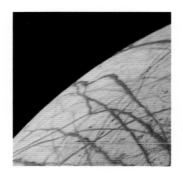

 # Glossary

amino acid—a substance found in the proteins and nucleic acids of all life on earth. Amino acids have been found, too, in certain meteorites and may occur throughout the universe

ammonia—a gas that makes up a small part of the atmospheres of the outer planets, from Jupiter to Pluto. Long ago, ammonia in the earth's atmosphere was important in the making of the first living things

asteroids—large rocks, a few hundred yards to a few hundred miles across, that go around the sun

atmosphere—the layer of gases above the surface of a planet or moon

billion—a thousand million. Written as 1,000,000,000

carbon—a substance that, because it links together in huge chains and rings, can form the complicated materials needed for life

carbonaceous chondrite —a rare type of meteorite

that is very old and contains simple carbon substances. These may include amino acids

carbon dioxide—the main gas in the atmospheres of Venus and Mars. On Earth, it is the gas that plants breathe in and that animals breathe out

cell—the smallest living part of an animal or plant. Human beings have billions of cells, each performing a certain task

Galaxy—the star city in which we live. It contains more than 100 billion stars and measures about 100,000 light-years across

galaxy—a star city. There are billions of galaxies throughout space

giant—an unusually large star. Giants may be young and hot, or old and cool

gravity—the force by which all objects pull on all other objects. Gravity is what keeps the planets moving around the sun

helium—the second

lightest substance of all and one that is found in the atmospheres of the outer planets

hydrogen—the lightest substance of all and the one that makes up most of the atmospheres of the frozen outer worlds

infrared rays—the kind of waves that carry heat. They are given off by all warm objects

light year—the distance traveled by light in one year. It is equal to about 6 trillion miles (9½ trillion kilometers)

meteorite—a rock from space that strikes the earth's surface

methane—a poisonous gas found in small amounts in the atmospheres of the outer planets. Like hydrogen and ammonia, it was also an important gas in the earth's early atmosphere

million—a thousand thousand. Written as 1,000,000

molecular cloud—a very large cloud of gas and dust in space from which new stars may form. Molecular clouds have been shown to contain small amounts of simple carbon substances, such as alcohol
molten—made into a liquid or fused together by intense heat
moon—a small world that circles around a planet

nitrogen—the most common gas in the earth's atmosphere

nucleic acids—very complicated substances found in all living things on earth. They store the information needed for life, and for living things to make copies of themselves

oxygen—a gas, making up about one-fifth of the earth's atmosphere, that humans and all other animals breathe
ozone—a gas, made from oxygen by the sun's ultraviolet rays, that forms a protective layer high in

the atmosphere

probe—a spacecraft designed to follow a certain path, gather information, and send it back to scientists on earth

proteins—very complicated substances, built from chains of amino acids, that are found in all living things on earth

radio telescope—an instrument used by astronomers for picking up radio waves—weak rays of energy—from space. It is usually much larger than an ordinary telescope

red dwarf—a small, cool, faint type of star. Red dwarfs are very common but none can be seen without a large telescope

silicon—a substance similar to carbon. Scientists have suggested that some forms of life could be based on it

solar system—the part of space in which we live. It includes the sun and all of the

objects that travel around it

supergiant—the largest type of star. Supergiants may be young and very hot, or old and cool

trillion—a thousand billion. Written as 1,000,000,000,000

ultraviolet rays—powerful waves of energy given off by very hot objects, such as stars. Though few ultraviolet rays from the sun reach the earth's surface, they can still cause sunburn

water vapor—the gas that forms from water. It is in the atmospheres of most of the planets, including earth

wavelength—the distance between two neighboring crests of a wave. Light, radio waves, and other types of energy that reach us from space can be measured in terms of their wavelength

X rays—waves of energy similar to light or radio waves, but much more powerful

 # **Suggested Reading**

Asimov, Isaac. *Extraterrestrial Civilizations*. New York:
    Crown, 1979.
"Are we alone?" this book begins by asking. The following
chapters then explore, in detail, the chances for intelligent
life in space and how we may meet or learn to communicate
with it. (Advanced)

"Extraterrestrials: The Great Debate." *Odyssey*, August
    1983, pp. 4-17.
How common is intelligent life in our galaxy? This article
explains the famous "Drake equation" and how it can be
used to give some possible answers. (Beginner-Intermediate)

Goldsmith, Donald, and Owen, Tobias. *The Search for Life
    in the Universe*. Menlo Park, Cal.: Benjamin-Cummings,
    1980.
Written by two scientists, this very thorough book covers all
topics to do with life in space, from biology to astronomy
and future spaceflight. (Advanced)

McBride, Ken. "Looking for Extrasolar Planets." *Astronomy*, October 1984, pp. 6-22.
For there to be other life, there must be planets going around other stars. This article shows how scientists are trying to find worlds outside the solar system, and the success they have had to date. (Advanced)

Other books in the Discovering Our Universe series that you may wish to refer to include: *The Sun: Our Neighborhood Star, The Planets: The Next Frontier, Where Are We Going in Space? and Stars: From Birth to Black Hole.*

Index

Age of the Dinosaurs, 23
amino acids, 16, 31
ammonia, 16, 27, 31, 33
Apollo spacecraft, 22
asteroids, 14, 21
atmosphere, 15, 17, 22-26, 30,
    32-34

Barnard's Star, 37
Beta Pictoris, 38
"brown dwarf," 39

carbon, 29, 31-32
carbonaceous chrondite, 31
carbon dioxide, 15, 17, 23-24
cells, 29
comets, 21

Drake, Frank, 43
Dyson, Freeman, 45

earth: life on, 19, 27, 29-32, 34,
    41, 47; solar system and,
    21-22, 32, 38, 43; surface
    of, 13-15, 24, 33

Epsilon Eridani, 37, 39, 43
Europa, 34-35

Formaulhaut, 38

Galaxy, the, 39, 41
giants, 41
gravity, 14, 25, 30, 33, 37

helium, 27
hydrogen, 27, 33

Infrared Astronomy Satellite,
    38
infrared rays, 45

Jupiter, 27, 33-35, 37-38, 41

light-years, 37, 44
Lowell, Percival, 25

Mariner 10, 22
Mars, 24-27, 32
Martians, 25
Mercury, 22-23, 32

meteorites, 31-32
meteors, 21
methane, 16, 27, 33, 47
molecular clouds, 31
moon, 21-22, 32, 41
"Moon bugs," 22
moons, 14, 21, 34

nitrogen, 15
nucleic acids, 16, 29, 31-32

oxygen, 17, 19, 24
ozone, 17

Pioneer 10, 44
planets, 14, 21, 27, 32, 38-39, 41
Pluto, 27, 47
proteins, 16, 29, 31-32

radio waves, 43
red dwarfs, 41

silicon, 31
61 Cygni, 37

solar system, 21, 31, 32, 34-35, 38-39, 43-44
star city, 13, 39
stars, 13, 31, 37-39, 41, 43
sun: formation of, 14; solar system and, 21-25, 32-33, 35, 37, 39, 41; ultraviolet rays and, 15, 17
supergiants, 41

Tau Ceti, 37, 39, 43

ultraviolet rays, 15-17, 43

Van Biesbroeck 8, 38
Vega, 38
Venus, 23-24, 32
Viking spacecraft, 26
volcanoes, 15, 24, 47
Voyager 1 and 2, 34, 44

water vapor, 15, 24, 33

X rays, 43